NEW ZEALAND
LAND OF LIGHT AND COLOUR

PHOTOGRAPHS, TEXT & LAYOUT
BY
PETER MORATH

FirstClass Publications

NEW ZEALAND
LAND OF LIGHT AND COLOUR

ISBN 0-908973-09-8

Photography and Text by Peter Morath

Photographs © Peter Morath
Publication © First Class Publications Ltd.

First published in 1997 by First Class Publications Ltd.
P.O. Box 6936, Wellesley Street, Auckland 1, New Zealand.

Printed by Colorcraft Ltd, Hong Kong.

DEDICATION

To my dear wife Shirley, for her constant patience, help and good advice. Also in loving memory of
my mother Sophie, in gratitude for a lifetime of encouragement.

ACKNOWLEDGMENTS

My thanks to Allan Fone and his team at New Zealand Photocorp, Christchurch, for many years of
film processing to a very high standard.

FirstClass Publications

Facing page: Lake Tekapo, Canterbury

NEW ZEALAND
LAND OF LIGHT AND COLOUR

New Zealand

NORTH ISLAND

Cape Reinga
Kaitaia
Kerikeri
Paihia
Opononi
WHANGAREI
Dargaville
Warkworth
Coromandel
AUCKLAND
Whitianga
Thames
Waihi
HAMILTON
TAURANGA
Otorohanga
ROTORUA
Whakatane
Te Kuiti
Tokoroa
Taupo
GISBORNE
Turangi
NEW PLYMOUTH
National Park
NAPIER
Waiouru
HASTINGS
WANGANUI
Bulls
Levin
PALMERSTON NORTH
Masterton
Upper Hutt
Takaka
WELLINGTON
NELSON
Picton
Blenheim
Westport
Greymouth
Kaikoura
Hokitika
Arthurs Pass
Franz Josef
CHRISTCHURCH
Mount Cook
Tekapo
Ashburton
SOUTH ISLAND
Milford Sound
TIMARU
Wanaka
Queenstown
Oamaru
Te Anau
Alexandra
DUNEDIN
INVERCARGILL
Bluff
STEWART ISLAND

Contents

INTRODUCTION

New Zealand began its existence about 100 million years ago when it gradually started to drift away from the great southern continent Gondwana. It remained without human visitation until around 900 A.D. when, legend has it, the first of the Polynesian explorers arrived.

Archeological evidence indicates that Maori settlement became established around 1300. The first Maori hunted the enormous flightless moa and founded a strong, warlike tribal society steeped in legend. Theirs was a culture of almost stone-age simplicity. They had no written language and metal was unknown to them. Their art took the form of wood and greenstone carving of great sensitivity and they practised fine oratory.

Europeans started to arrive in small numbers after James Cook's first landing in 1769, but it was not until the early 1840s that large scale European immigration began. Settlers found a wild and undeveloped land of great beauty and diversity. In the North Island emerald bays with white-sand beaches contrasted with the stark, volcanic Central Plateau. In the South Island the contrasts were equally great, with the Main Divide separating lush rain forest in the west from vast, dry plains in the east.

Since their arrival much has changed. The land has been tamed, large cities built and modern technology and communication introduced. While the jet-age has brought New Zealand much closer to the rest of the world, its geographic isolation has ensured that it remains virtually free of the atmospheric pollution of more populous continents. Its skies retain a rare clarity that enables the scenic magnificence to be enjoyed to the full and for it truly to be judged a 'land of light and colour'.

The
NORTH ISLAND

New Zealand has a population of about 3.7 million people. 75% live in the North Island, as do 89% of Maori, who represent 13% of the country's citizens.

The first European immigrants arrived in 1814, when missionaries established a settlement in the Bay of Islands. Today the Bay is renowned for its big-game fishing and idyllic beaches and is the region's major tourist centre. Northland's industries include oil refining (near its city of Whangarei), farming, fishing and forestry, although the few remaining giant kauri trees in the far north are now protected.

Auckland is home to over a quarter of New Zealand's population. It is recognised as the country's commercial capital and has the largest Polynesian population anywhere in the Pacific. This rapidly expanding city is beautifully located on the Waitemata Harbour and within easy reach are the islands of the Hauraki Gulf and the bush-clad mountains and fine beaches of the Waitakeres Ranges and Coromandel Peninsula.

To the south is the Waikato region with its thriving dairy industry. Hamilton, its provincial centre, is the country's fourth largest city.

The Bay of Plenty is the heart of the kiwifruit industry and the port of Tauranga handles more export cargo than any other in New Zealand. This includes much of the timber grown in the vast forests of the central North Island.

The thermal areas of Rotorua, Taupo and the Tongariro National Park provide the North Island's most spectacular sights. Among these are geysers, boiling mud pools and active volcanoes. In winter Mount Ruapehu's ski-fields are an added attraction.

Eastland is sparsely populated and includes the unspoilt Urewera National Park. There is fine coastal scenery around the East Cape north of Gisborne.

Napier and Hastings are the twin cities of the highly productive Hawke's Bay region. Fruit and vegetable growing are major industries, as are wine-making and sheep farming.

Taranaki is famous for dairy farming and also for the production of natural gas and synthetic fuel. The city of New Plymouth is dominated by the beautiful, symmetrical, snow-capped Mount Taranaki in the Egmont National Park.

To the south and south-east lie the predominantly pastoral regions of Wanganui, with its scenic and historic river, Manawatu, with its university city of Palmerston North and Wairarapa, well known for the Golden Shears sheep-shearing contest held at Masterton.

Wellington has been New Zealand's capital since 1865. It is the country's second largest city, with satellite towns in the Hutt Valley to the north. It has a magnificent natural harbour from which ferries operate to the South Island.

Facing page: Roberton Island, Bay of Islands.
Right: Kerikeri Inlet, Bay of Islands.

Opua is the Bay's principal port. It provides moorings for some of the many boats that sail here during the summer months.

BAY OF ISLANDS

Steeped in history, Russell is probably the most beautiful of all the area's resorts
and can be reached by car ferry from Opua.

BAY OF ISLANDS

Sheltered Bay has one of the many lovely beaches on the Tutukaka Coast, a short distance east of Whangarei.

NORTHLAND

These boats are moored at Whangarei, the regional centre. The city has a busy port and a very scenic peninsula nearby.

NORTHLAND

Crimson flowered pohutukawa trees are a much loved feature of the Christmas period in the north. They are seen here in full bloom at Oneroa Bay on Waiheke Island.

HAURAKI GULF

Mansion House Bay on Kawau Island is a favourite destination for boat trips from Auckland and Sandspit near Warkworth.

HAURAKI GULF

Piha is one of several fine surfing beaches on the coast to the west of Auckland.

WAITAKERES

The central business district overlooks the Waitemata Harbour, with the Hauraki Gulf and Rangitoto Island beyond.

AUCKLAND

Pohutukawa trees frame this view of the Harbour Bridge, seen from Stokes Point
on the North Shore.

AUCKLAND

The city's Maritime Museum offers many interesting
exhibits from the region's nautical past.

AUCKLAND

The lights of the Harbour Bridge shimmer in the calm waters of Westhaven Marina.

AUCKLAND

The colourful lights of the city refect in the harbour at dusk.

AUCKLAND

Cows graze contentedly on the summit of Mount Eden, only a short distance from the
bustle of the city centre.

AUCKLAND

The symmetrical cone of Rangitoto Island is a familiar part of the Auckland landscape and can be seen to advantage from Okahu Bay.

AUCKLAND

Te Horo Rock stands guard over lovely Cathedral Cove, north of Hahei on the east coast of the peninsula

COROMANDEL

Cathedral Cove, named after its huge natural arch, has a popular picnic beach.

COROMANDEL

Mount Paku at Tairua offers a pleasant walk and panoramic views along the coast.

COROMANDEL

Tairua is one of the peninsula's most attractive resorts. Its harbour is seen here at sunset.

COROMANDEL

Owharoa Falls are a feature of Karangahake Gorge, once a major gold mining area.
Right: Whangamata is another very popular holiday resort on the peninsula's east coast.

COROMANDEL

Mount Maunganui, with its magnificent Ocean Beach, guards the entrance to Tauranga Harbour.
Right: White Island, 50km offshore, is one of the country's three active volcanoes.

BAY OF PLENTY

Government Gardens offers a blaze of floral colour, fine bowling greens and a museum
and art gallery in the Bathhouse.

ROTORUA

Fairy and Rainbow Springs are one of the city's top attractions. A stream
meanders beside a tranquil bush track within the park.

ROTORUA

Mount Tarawera is seen beyond Lake Okareka, one of several attractive lakes in the area.
Left: When the mountain errupted in 1886, the explosion left this huge crater.

ROTORUA

The colourful and effervescent Champagne Pool at Waiotapu.

Pohutu Geyser at Whakarewarewa, Rotorua's most spectacular sight.

ROTORUA

Boiling mud pools at Whakarewarewa.

The Warbrick Terrace in the Waimangu Thermal Valley.

ROTORUA

Maori women demonstrate cooking in a hot pool at Whakarewarewa, one of the many interesting features of this world famous thermal area.

ROTORUA

Maori Carving at Whakarewarewa.

Maori girl with carving at Ohinemutu.

Top: Poi dancing at Ohinemutu.
Bottom: The wero or challenge at Whakarewrewa

ROTORUA

The Papakorito Falls are one of several impressive waterfalls that flow into Lake Waikaremoana.

EASTLAND

Lake Waikaremoana has a wild beauty and its extensive waters are enclosed by vast areas
of unspoilt native bush.

EASTLAND

Fishing boats await their next duty in Gisborne's busy harbour.
Left: These cabbage trees are at Tolaga Bay on the East Cape north of Gisborne, an area with fine coastal scenery.

EASTLAND

Tree ferns and nikau palms are among examples of the native plants that can be seen at Morere Springs north of Wairoa.

EASTLAND

Wine producing is a major industry in this region. Te Mata estate near Hastings
is one of the many vineyards.

HAWKE'S BAY

Cape Kidnappers, east of Napier, has a large nesting colony of gannets. Organised visits enable the public to approach very close to the birds.

HAWKE'S BAY

The city of Napier is well known for the Art Deco style of architecture used in its reconstruction following the 1931 earthquake.

HAWKE'S BAY

Magnificent coastal scenery can be enjoyed from the White Cliffs Walkway near Tongaporutu.
Right: The Shapely 2518m cone of dormant volcano Mount Taranaki reflects in the waters of Lake Mangamahoe, near New Plymouth.

TARANAKI

Active volcano Mount Ngauruhoe (2291m) dominates this view of Tongariro National Park.
To the left are Mount Tongariro and Lake Taupo.

TONGARIRO

Mount Ruapehu (2797m) is the North Island's highest mountain, and is another active volcano.
It is also the Island's main skiing centre.

TONGARIRO

The Wanganui River is at its most beautiful in its upper reaches. Jetboat and riverboat trips
operate from the city of Wanganui.

WANGANUI

This aerial view north of the city shows Paremata, Mana, Plimmerton and Porirua Harbour, with Kapiti Island in the distance.

WELLINGTON

The high-rise buildings of Jervois Quay are reflected in the calm harbour waters near the rowing club and Frank Kitts Park.
Right: Wellington's claim to having one of the finest harbours in the world is easily justified when it is viewed from the air.

WELLINGTON

The rising sun is reflected in the windows of the city's buildings beyond
Clyde Quay Marina.

WELLINGTON

Mount Victoria is a favourite place from which to view the capital city,
especially at dusk.

WELLINGTON

A ride on the cable-car up to Kelburn is very popular with visitors and residents alike.
The trip offers extensive views of city and harbour.

WELLINGTON

Civic Square is the city's chief focal point for the arts. The Michael Fowler Centre is the principal concert hall.

WELLINGTON

The
SOUTH ISLAND

In 1842 Nelson became the South Island's first region to receive immigrants from Britain in large numbers. Much hard work was required to clear the land, but they had come to a bountiful area. Nelson and its neighbouring province of Marlborough enjoy more sunshine than anywhere else in the country. Today the region produces vines, hops and timber in abundance. Marlborough makes world class wines and the magic of its Sounds competes with Nelson's golden beaches to attract holiday makers.

The pace of life on the West Coast is much more leisurely now than during the frenetic gold rushes of the 1860s. Timber is the main industry and coal is still mined, mainly for exporting. Greymouth and Westport have active fishing fleets, and there is farming along the fertile coastal strip. The scenery has unique beauty, with the country's highest peaks reflecting in placid lakes and verdant native bush sweeping down to meet the pounding surf of the Tasman Sea.

Canterbury, the country's largest province, lies to the east of the Main Divide. Its tussock-covered foothills and vast plains present a strong contrast to the visitor arriving from the forested west. This is farming country on a grand scale and, not surprisingly, agriculture is the largest of the region's diverse industries. Much of the country's electricity is generated by the hydro lakes in the Mackenzie Basin in the south, above which tower some of New Zealand's highest mountains. Christchurch is the provincial centre and the third largest city in the country. There the English influence is very strong, exemplified in such activities as punting on the Avon River.

The gold rushes of the 1860s reached their peak in the central areas of Otago. As a result, Dunedin became the most populated city in the country for a time. Today it is the second largest urban area in the South Island, with a strong Scottish heritage and much fine Victorian architecture. The scenic peninsula nearby has the only mainland nesting site in the world of the royal albatross. Queenstown is the Island's main tourist destination, and Central Otago has some magnificent mountain and lake scenery which looks its best in autumn.

Southland is another major farming region. Its main city of Invercargill is not far from a large aluminium smelter near Bluff, a port renowned for its oysters. From Bluff a ferry operates to beautiful Stewart Island, the most southerly of the country's three main Islands.

Fiordland National Park is a magnificent, unspoilt, wilderness area with unequalled walks, including the world famous Milford Track. For those who are less energetic, the grandeur of Milford Sound provides a fitting climax to any visit to New Zealand.

Facing Page: Bruce Bay, Westland
Right: Punchbowl Falls, Arthur's Pass, Canterbury.

Breaker Bay near Kaiteriteri has a beautiful, sheltered beach with
easy access and safe bathing.

NELSON

Kaiteriteri has one of the finest beaches in the South Island. The lovely golden sand is a feature of this part of the country.

NELSON

Abel Tasman National Park has fine walking tracks and many delightful bays with golden beaches, as seen here at Torrent Bay.

NELSON

Motueka is one of the country's major fruit growing areas. The neatly fenced orchards can be seen in this aerial view towards the west.

NELSON

The huge Archway Islands are a short distance offshore from the beautiful beach at
Wharariki, south of Farewell Spit.

NELSON

This unique rock formation is at Totaranui in the Abel Tasman National Park.
Camping is a popular pastime in this area.

NELSON

Sheltered Beck's Bay on Queen Charlotte Sound makes a peaceful mooring place.
Left: Luxuriant tree ferns border the road to Tennyson Inlet.

MARLBOROUGH

The complex nature of the Marlbourough Sounds coastline can be fully appreciated only from a high altitude.
Right: The colourful crystallising ponds of the salt works at Lake Grassmere near Blenheim.

MARLBOROUGH

Picton on Queen Charlotte Sound is the region's most popular holiday resort and
a superb location for boating.

MARLBOROUGH

Kaikoura has a wonderful combination of mountain and marine scenery. Whale watching
trips are operated from the township.

MARLBOROUGH

Known as "The Pancake Rocks" these formations are located at Punakaiki, between Greymouth and Westport.

BULLER

Woodpecker Bay south of Westport has a fine stand of nikau palms to welcome the incoming Tasman rollers.

BULLER

The Motukiekie Rocks north of Greymouth are one of several similar formations on the West Coast.
Right: Fox Glacier névé with the majestic backdrop of Mounts Cook and Tasman.

WESTLAND

Lake Matheson is renowned for its mirror-like reflections of the two highest peaks in New Zealand: Mount Cook on the right and Mount Tasman on the left.
Left: Lake Mapourika near Franz Josef reflects some of the major peaks of the Main Divide in its calm waters.

WESTLAND

This autumn scene is at Waiau in north Canterbury which is a very productive farming area.

CANTERBURY

The Waiau River, flowing beneath the Ferry Bridge near Hanmer Springs,
is popular for jetboating.

CANTERBURY

Sand bars form an intricate pattern in this aerial view of the
Ashley River mouth east of Rangiora.

CANTERBURY

The rolling hills of the Motunau area of north Canterbury make ideal
sheep grazing country.

CANTERBURY

Hoar frost enhances this view at Cass, on the main highway to Arthur's Pass.

CANTERBURY

Another wintry scene unfolds as the sun rises above Methven and Mount Hutt.

CANTERBURY

Both blue borage (above) and
Sunflowers (right) grow in
abundance at Methven.

CANTERBURY

Above: Tulips are grown commercially at Springston.
Left: Fields of rape near Ashburton.

CANTERBURY

Mount Hutt, a popular skiing resort, overlooks the Rakaia River and gorge.

CANTERBURY

A huge pohutukawa tree dwarfs this homestead at the small settlement of French Farm on Banks Peninsula.

CANTERBURY

Akaroa was a French settlement for a short time from 1840 before passing into British hands.
Left: An aerial view of Akaroa Harbour.

CANTERBURY

Lyttelton Harbour offers excellent sailing, and the area boasts several yacht clubs.

CANTERBURY

Evening light catches the port of Lyttelton and enhances the contours of
Banks Peninsula's mountains beyond.

CANTERBURY

Snow lies deep on the mountains of Banks Peninsula in this view from
Governor's Bay on Lyttelton Harbour.

CANTERBURY

The "North West Arch", seen here from New Brighton, is a frequent feature of Canterbury's weather.

CHRISTCHURCH

Hagley Park, near the city centre, is at its loveliest in early spring.
Right: Punting on the Avon River is a relaxing, and very British, pastime.

CHRISTCHURCH

One of the city's popular restored trams passes Victoria Square.

CHRISTCHURCH

Worcester Boulevard and The Arts Centre are places of great activity,
particularly on fine weekends.

CHRISTCHURCH

Hot-air balloons often fly from Hagley Park. This scene shows the annual Balloon Festival, held in mid-winter.

CHRISTCHURCH

This fine avenue of poplars lines the Avon River between Manchester and Madras Streets.

CHRISTCHURCH

The colourful scene on a mid-winter's evening from the Price
Waterhouse building, the city's highest.

CHRISTCHURCH

Cathedral Square, seen here at dusk, is traditionally accepted to be the centre of the city.

CHRISTCHURCH

The Church of the Good Shepherd stands at the southern end of Lake Tekapo.
Right: Lake Alexandrina is close to Lake Tekapo.

CANTERBURY LAKES

Silver birch trees line the main highway to Central Otago,
skirting the shore of Lake Pukaki.

CANTERBURY LAKES

Larch trees, seen here in autumn, border the lake along the road to Mount Cook at Ferintosh.

CANTERBURY LAKES

Motorists bound for Mount Cook often encounter flocks of sheep being driven along the road.

MOUNT COOK

The entrance to Glentanner sheep station is an ideal place from which to view Mount Cook.

MOUNT COOK

Mount Cook (3753m), with the Tasman Glacier at its base and, to its right, Mount Tasman (3498m).
Right: Ski-plane trips onto the glaciers are a great feature of the area. This aircraft is flying near the Hochstetter ice-fall.

MOUNT COOK

Wild lupins make a blaze of colour near the Hermitage in the summertime.
Right: One of the finest experiences to be enjoyed in New Zealand is a flight around Mount Cook at sunset.

MOUNT COOK

Lake Benmore is one of the country's main hydro lakes. In this view the dam can be seen in the foreground.

WAITAKI

Huge clay cliffs tower above the Ahuriri River valley near Omarama.

WAITAKI

The foreshore of Lake Wanaka is a colourful place for an autumn picnic.

CENTRAL OTAGO

The Southern Alps provide a fine backdrop for the township of Wanaka
and its Picturesque lake.

CENTRAL OTAGO

Glendhu Bay on Lake Wanaka is close to the Mount Aspiring National Park.
Right: Mount Aspiring (3040m), although actually in Westland, is more closely associated with the Wanaka area.

CENTRAL OTAGO

The Kawarau Gorge was one of the region's main gold mining areas.

CENTRAL OTAGO

The Crown Road from Wanaka to Queenstown provides magnificent views over the Arrow Basin.

CENTRAL OTAGO

The northern side of The Remarkables range rises above this autumn scene near Speargrass Flat.

CENTRAL OTAGO

This spring scene near Arrowtown is dominated by Double Cone (2343m), the summit of
The Remarkables range

CENTRAL OTAGO

Pony trekkers cross the Arrow River at Arrowtown.

CENTRAL OTAGO

Arrowtown was one of the main gold prospecting centres in the 1860s. Now the visitors come for the gold of its trees, not that of its riverbed.

CENTRAL OTAGO

Sheep graze at Lake Hayes, close to Arrowtown , one of the scenic gems of this region.

CENTRAL OTAGO

Artists try to capture the autumn delights of Lake Hayes in the late afternoon.

CENTRAL OTAGO

Jetboating on the Kawarau River is a great tourist attraction in this area.

QUEENSTOWN

The Shotover River jetboat is about to pass under the Edith Cavell Bridge.

QUEENSTOWN

A trip on Lake Wakatipu on the old steamer "Earnslaw" is a great favourite with visitors.
Right: The Skyline Gondola offers its riders panoramic views of the town, the lake and The Remarkables range.

QUEENSTOWN

Glenorchy, at the head of Lake Wakatipu, with Mount Earnslaw (2819m)
and the Dart River mouth.

QUEENSTOWN

Coronet Peak skifield is one of the region's major winter attractions.

QUEENSTOWN

Carey's Bay is close to Port Chalmers, the region's main port.

DUNEDIN

The walkway to Tunnel Beach provides fine views of cliffs, rock formations and the pounding surf.

DUNEDIN

The Octagon, flanked by the cathedral, townhall and council offices, is the city's principal focal point.

DUNEDIN

The University of Otago is one of Dunedin's finest examples of Victorian architecture.

DUNEDIN

Riverton, west of Invercargill, is a fishing port with a history dating back to the days of whaling.
Left: Purakaunui Falls, near Owaka in South Otago, is one of the main attractions of the Catlins area.

SOUTHLAND

Lake Te Anau on a fine spring morning (above) contrasts sharply with a view in the same direction as hail showers sweep across the Murchison Mountains (left).

FIORDLAND

Cabbage trees frame The Lion and Pembroke Glacier at Milford Sound.
Right: The Sutherland Falls are one of the worlds highest waterfalls at 580.3 metres.

FIORDLAND

Mitre Peak at Milford Sound is one of New Zealand's best known landmarks.

FIORDLAND

No visit to Milford would be complete without a boat trip along the Sound.

FIORDLAND